Trusting The Go

The
Next Best
Thing

Table Of Contents

IISBN-13:978-1493567171

Copyright Marnie L. Thomson 2013

Forward

Every poem in this small booklet
Took just minutes as it came
And was inspired by the Scriptures
That extol the Saviour's Name.
He's the King of kings, Creator
Sovereign Lord and Prince of Peace
Yet He tends us like a Shepherd
I know, for I am one He leads.

Hebrews 13:20,21
*Now may the God of peace who brought again
From the dead our Lord Jesus,
the great shepherd of the sheep
by the blood of the eternal covenant
equip you with everything good
that you may do his will,
working in us that which is pleasing in his sight,
through Jesus Christ,
to whom be glory forever and ever. Amen*

The Good Shepherd Provides

The Next Best Thing

All things work out for the good
Of those who love You Lord
Nothing that we come upon
Can sever that strong cord
Of love that binds our hearts to Yours
You knit our hearts as one
And we are safe within the bond
Until our days are done
And with this promise You include
A chorus we can sing
That every moment yet to come
Will be the next best thing.
Best for our hearts to learn to trust
Each step you lead us through
For everything ahead of us
Brings us closer to You
So not just for the blessing past
Of even for today
But every future moment
Is a kindness on its way.

Romans 8:28
*And we know that for those who love God
all things work together for good,
for those who are called
according to His purpose.*

Four Friends

Four friends winding down the road of life
Each a mother, sister, daughter, wife
Each one trying to do the best she can
Friendship part of Your most precious plan.
Sometimes one encounters valleys low
Stands still, no idea where to go
Three hearts call out for their Shepherd's aid
Spirits lifted as the burden's laid
Great gifts flowing from God's throne of grace
They find God's mercy in each friend's embrace
Each one steadied by these cords of love
Hold them nearer to God's heart above.

Proverbs 17:17
*A friend loves at all times,
and a brother is born for adversity.*

On trusting the Good Shepherd

Not

Not as expected, not as I planned
Not what I pictured from where I now stand
Not as I wished for, not what I thought
Not upon not upon not upon not.
Bigger and better and smaller and worse
Easier, harder, a blessing, a curse
Not what it seemed that others have had
So much of it happy, so much of it sad
All these ideas however they came
Nothing and nobody turned out the same.
You are the Potter, I am just clay
Whatever it seemed would be coming my way
Was bigger and better. It's harder, it's slow.
I know You'll complete it. That's all that I know.

James 4:14
Yet you do not know what tomorrow will bring.
What is your life: for you are a mist
that appears for a little time and then vanishes.

Signs and Symptoms of The State of Grace

I never, ever came to You
When You were not enough
When You ignored my pleading
Or said, "Sorry life is tough
And you have made this bed you hate,
So sit there. I don't care.
You only got what you deserve.
Who said that life is fair?"
I never ever turned to You
And found that You had left
And I was simply there alone,
Frightened, lost, bereft
With Your number disconnected
And Your email address changed
Spinning wildly in a world,
Gravity all re-arranged.
No, every time I look for You,
You are more than I could hope
More gracious and compassionate,
More than just some way to cope

So much bigger, so much stronger,
More than ever I conceive.
And those things I'd been preferring
Make my waking up heart grieve.
And You truly are a Gentleman
Who lets me choose the road
So I can go on wallowing
And carrying my load
Or turn to You, relinquish
And take action when You speak
Trust You to know what's best for me,
Even though I am so weak.
You say, "If you really love Me,
I will know as you obey
Without fear you'll simply follow,
Learn to trust the words I say.
Perfect love is never fearful
For it knows the Master's heart."
Gentle Shepherd, Good Kind Father,
I can follow Who You are.

1 John 4:18
There is no fear in love, but perfect love casts out fear.
For fear has to do with punishment and
whoever fears has not been perfected in love.

Sometimes The Day

Sometimes the day grows grim and bleak
And I feel lost, alone and weak
Without the strength to push ahead
My soul is filled with fear and dread
As every manmade institute
Fails me and leaves me destitute
And so I know the only thing
To count on is my Reigning King
And as the skies all blacken down
No bird to sing, no hopeful sound
I know the only way for me
Lies in Your gracious sovereignty
Like storm clouds that I know will burst
My heart cries out in raging thirst
To hear Your voice and see Your hand
And watch as You give that command
And so You strip away the part
That shades Your goodness from my heart
And I am left to watch and see
More kindness that You've done for me.
Then humbled in the mighty wave
And shaken by the gift You gave
Commit my heart on bended knee
To live my life still more for Thee.

Isaiah 30:18
Therefore the Lord waits to be gracious to you,
and therefore he exalts himself to show mercy to you.
For the Lord is a God of justice; blessed are all those who wait for him.

On trusting the Good Shepherd

Blessed

Here I sit with blessings heaping
In this hour before I'm sleeping
Just reviewing all You've done
In one rotation, earth and sun
Here I'm blessed beyond all measure
Filled to full with Your good pleasure
O so rich beyond my saying
At Your feet them I am laying
Thank You for this happy day
When with zeal I loudly say
You are all my strength and power
So I thank You in this hour
Times have been when I was weary
Nights stood still and days were dreary
But for now the morning's come
I find blessings one on one.
I can never speak my heart
For the kindness You impart
So I humbly bow and say
Thank You Lord for this, today.

Isaiah 63:7
*I will recount the steadfast love of the Lord,
the praises of the Lord, according to all
that the Lord has granted us and the great goodness
to the house of Israel that he has granted them
according to his compassion, according
to the abundance of his steadfast love.*

Wait For Light

O so cold with ice and snow
Water frozen, cars won't go
And underneath it all still lies
The everlasting arms and eyes
That see our trouble, hear our cries
No plea too weak, no cry too loud
No pressure muffled by the crowd
Of other cries that rise to Thee
Your arms still reach, Your eyes still see
And nothing in my little space
Escapes Your mercy or Your grace
And sometimes it is good and right
To curl up small and wait for light
You understand my feeble frame
So here I wait and breathe Your name.

Psalm 130:5,6
I wait for the Lord, my soul waits, and in his word I hope;
My soul waits for the Lord more than
the watchmen wait for the morning,
more than the watchmen wait for the morning.

Our Group

Since you each were so determined
That your little books were signed
I worked it out collectively
I didn't think you'd mind

When I think of Sara, I always think of laughter
And then I think of kindness immediately after
When I think of Rachel I think of joy and fun
If I needed cheering up I know she'd be the one
If I need encouragement, Beth springs to my mind
She lives life with compassion, that is what I always find
Jim is more a quiet one, he's witty and he's wise
And Barb shows gentle beauty, they work well side by side
Bill shows us discernment, like wise Bereans did with Paul
He lines things up with Scripture, very noble all in all
Maureen's a loving spirit, persevering day by day
She's a brave and godly soldier. I see her that way.
Now Bruce, he loves to learn things and apply them to his life
And in this you must believe me, for I'm that fellow's wife
So that's the group God gave us, we are family in the Lord
And when this study's finished, every Monday I'll be bored.

With love in Christ
Marina

Dawn

I am far too rich
I have way too much
I have seen Your hand
I have felt Your touch.
I saw morning born
With compassions new
Mercies streaming down
With a heavy dew
And creation stood
With its breath held still
Then it sang to You
Of Your perfect will.
The unveiling of
Your most tender heart
And the wonder of
My own little part.
I am loved by You
For Your own Name's sake
I'm a glistening wave
On a crystal lake.

Psalm 98:7,8
Let the sea roar, and all that fills it;
the world and those who dwell in it!
Let the rivers clap their hands;
let the hills sing in joy together.

New Year's Eve

End of another year now looms
As one more year slips by
And here we sit rejoicing
That we saw these day-gifts fly
And none of them brought grief to us
Though many brought us pain
But all of us have days ahead
To try our best again
To bow to You the Maker
And Creator of it all
The very God of very gods
Who rescues from the fall
And while we have no way to know
What lies ahead of us

We'll try to take it graciously,
Without complaint or fuss
So keep our hearts raised up in praise
And help our faith stand strong
So we can sing out loudly
If the nights grow dark and long
For You our Lord reign mightily,
Each moment in Your gaze
And all that's ours to give You
Is obedience and praise
Thank You that You give us hope
To live in victory.
Because of, in and through Your strength
Our soul success will be.

1 Samuel 7:12
*Then Samuel took a stone and set it up
between Mispah and Shen and called its name
Ebenezer, for he said, "Till now the Lord has helped us."*

Your Word

I read Your book again this year
And kneel in awe and holy fear
For all You've done and given me
Through Christ Your Son.
The tree of life that starts and ends
The book of life that names Your friends
The tree of death that brings us life
Through Christ Your Son
That Word Who humbly came to live
Who gave up all, yet came to give
The very God of very gods
Our Christ Your Son
Ten thousand glorious truths of You
Graze just the tip of all You do
Ten thousand ways I need to change
For Christ Your Son
This story much too rich to learn
Too dear to pay, too hard to earn
This story written in the blood
Of Christ Your Son
Unveil my eyes, replace this heart
Make every dawn another start
For me to only breathe out praise
For Christ Your Son.

Psalm 119:105
*You word is a lamp to my feet
and a light to my path.*

Hot Bright Sunny Day

Hot bright sunny sky
Here I sit and wonder why
I am blessed with so much good
I would shout it if I could
I sit here with over-much
I've heard Your voice, I've felt Your touch
Set here in a world gone mad
Can I share this joy I've had?
Let me rise and make a start
You the beat within my heart
Lead me, guide me that I do
Just those things You ask me to.
Much to do, the clock to fight
Seeds to sow before this night
Steps to walk with You before
Let me see You, clearer, more
Let me do this one day well
Those observing, clear to tell
Every step to every place
Only in Your love and grace.

Psalm 90:12
Teach us to number our days that we may get a heart of wisdom.

Quiet Calm

Quiet, calm, young green day
Trying to figure how to pray
What to bring before Your throne
World all Yours and none my own
None my own, my very breath
My life Your gift to conquer death
You gave Your life and still You give
In gratitude each breath I live
Let this be a holy day
Thoughts I think and words I say
All dressed up the tributes soar
Thankful, grateful evermore
Yours alone, the plan, the strength
Carry me though life's long length
Even so, today can be
My attempt, my offering
Slow me down, cause me to pause
Realizing that You're the cause
Of every good that life unfolds
All the silvers, all the golds
Praise to You my wondrous King
Shouts of joy my heart will sing
You the Lord of earth and sky
Mine to ever wonder why.

Psalm 8:4
*What is man that you are mindful of him,
and the son of man that you care for him?*

On trusting the Good Shepherd

Provisions

Peace comes pouring
For we know
That our Saviour
Loves us so.
Faith comes marching
In a world
Where the common
Comes unfurled.
Strength comes streaming
From Somewhere
Knowing that You
Meet us here.
Hope is flowing
Like a stream
Nothing here
As it would seem.
Love comes bubbling
Like a flood
Purchased with
The Saviour's blood.
Not an instant
Out of Gaze
Keeping us
Through nights and days.

Isaiah 26:3
You keep him in perfect peace
whose mind is stayed on you,
because he trusts in you

No Mistakes

You are Sovereign and Compassionate
And You do not make mistakes
This is not a game of chance we play
Not messing with the Fates.
You promise to make all things work
Together in Your Will
And though it takes our breath away
We trust You with this still.
You know that I would take his place
That makes more sense to me.
I know I must accept that things
Are how they're supposed to be.
You know how much this pierces them
You know the grief and pain

On trusting the Good Shepherd

You know we'll come to You for strength
Again, again, again.
O let no single moment
Of this story go to waste.
Stream Your tender sweet compassion.
Let them know and feel and taste
Your gentleness and goodness
Though it feels we can't endure
Let us know with hearts emboldened
That our faith in You stands sure.
Move in closer than our breathing
Shelter us under Your wing
May each sentence of this story
Of Your glorious mercy sing.

Hebrews 12:28
*Therefore let us be grateful for receiving a kingdom
that cannot be shaken,
and thus let us offer to God acceptable worship,
with reverence and awe*

Your Temple

When King Solomon built Your temple,
Filled with beauty, clothed in gold
It was still a world of wonder
That Your goodness it could hold
Lord God our King of Mercy,
Love and kindness moved Your heart
Every step toward us,
Purely gracious from the start
What You really longed for
Were those holy garden days
When You walked beside Your children
And they loved Your heart, Your ways
And through every page of history
The story's lead to this
We are lost, alone and broken
And the world has gone amiss
We have all marched in rebellion
Down dark roads we thought we knew
Every step and path and valley
Moving us away from You.
Yet, You kept on orchestrating
Symphonies we could not hear

From our first kiss of betrayal,
Through the cross, the nails, the spear
Love sang louder than the hatred,
Grace sang sweeter than the curse
And as only You could manage,
You composed the final verse.
Moving closer than a temple,
Now in human hearts You dwell
And You entrust us with Your story
To live and tell it well
And the End is the Beginning,
Earth and heaven new and bright
Lamb of God its glorious Lamp,
The nations walking in Your light
Hear Your people call for mercy,
Turn our hearts back to Your throne
Let us hear refrains of triumph,
Earth Your temple, Yours alone
Finally woven altogether
Into Your most precious best
From the Lamb Who bought our freedom
And our wandering hearts Your rest.

2 Chronicles 6:41
And now arise, O Lord God,
and go to your resting place,
you and the ark of your might.
Let your priests, O Lord God, be clothed with salvation,
and let your saints rejoice in your goodness.

About Expectatons

I don't expect with every storm
That knocks upon my door
I'll always find a rainbow
Painting colours on my floor
I don't expect that every
Diagnosis I receive
Will come with clear instructions
And all pain and grief will leave.
I don't expect that through my days
I won't encounter doubt
That causes me to wonder
What this life is all about.
I do expect a couple things,
Those things I know and trust
That time on earth is fleeting
And we all return to dust
But Jesus King and Conqueror
Shelters us with mighty hands
And someday all the madness will make sense,
We'll understand
That even through those valleys
When the road was hard to see
He was always close beside us
Leading on in victory.

1 Corinthians 15:57
But thanks be to God,
who gives us the victory
through our Lord Jesus Christ

On trusting the Good Shepherd

No More Questions

I've had some people tell me,
When they get to Heaven's door
They plan to ask You questions
Things they wished they knew before
And it makes me kind of wonder
They don't seem to realize
When we finally get to Heaven
We will see with different eyes.
For You say we'll be like Jesus
When we see Him face to face
Just a glimpse of Jesus' visage
Every question will erase
Your Holiness and Splendour
Majesty that shines like gold
So much vaster and much richer
Than earth-bound minds could ever hold.
No longer seeing dimly
We will fully comprehend
How You worked sanctification
Through the trials You chose to send.

1 John3:2
*Beloved, we are God's children now,
and what we will be has not yet appeared;
but we know that when he appears
we shall be like him because we shall see him
as he is.*

Blinders

Take off these blinders Lord
Help me to see
Unlimit my vision
From all that could be
Restricting perceptions
Of joy, hope and love
I need a fresh glimpse
To flow down from above.
Clear out my mind of
Those thoughts that confound
That blur and that smear
That distort what's around
That cause me to wonder
If it's worth all this mess
That makes my faith flounder
And my heart's peace flow less.
As I surrender dark
Thoughts to Your throne
Replace these ideas
With those of Your own
I need Your Spirit
To unchain my heart

I kneel and I ask
Reconstruction to start.
Unfetter, unbind, unleash
And set straight
And as You accomplish this
Teach me to wait
Thank You for fountains
Of mercies that flow
In streams of Your radiance
To Your children below
And our thanks You don't tire
Of directing Your sheep
As You shepherd us homeward,
Through long nights without sleep.
Thank You for victories
In battles unseen
Our thanks that You're sovereign
And always have been
Our praise that You're reigning
In every detail
That we're Yours and You
Never, no never will fail.

2 Corinthians 4:6
*For God, who said, "Let light shine out of darkness,"
has shone in our hearts
to give the light of the knowledge
of the glory of God in the face of Jesus Christ.*

The God You Are

I speak to You Father but I picture You wrong
Like I miss the lyrics of a beautiful song
Or I hear the rhythm from the orchestra pit
But I miss the play that goes along with it
I love You Father but my heart can't reach
Like a teaspoon of sand on the ocean's beach
Or a flashlight shining up at night's vast stars
I have just an inkling of the God You are.
You know me Father more than I can guess
And the part I do know I like less and less
For I fail so often with the words I say
And the thoughts I harbour any given day.
I know You Father hold me with Your arm
And through any weather I need fear no harm
For You clothe me Saviour with Your righteousness
And You see Your Jesus shining through my mess.
I love You deeper as I know You more
And I feel more restless than I have before
For that Day that's coming when Your earth's made new
And we join the angels as they worship You
I see Your radiance in so many things
As I catch those glimmers my heart always sings
For my great Redeemer Who has won the grave
When You left high Heaven and You chose to save.
You listen Father when I speak to You
And that's one more marvel in the things You do.

2 Corinthians 5:21
*For our sake he made him to be sin who knew no sin,
so that in him we might become the righteousness of God.*

My Shepherd

How aptly You call me
Your little lost lamb
And with such a great kindness
You say that I am
For sheep are defenseless
And helpless and slow
They only will follow
A Shepherd they know
They're fearful and sickly
And prone to disease
And they need their Shepherd
To heal and set free
I am grateful dear Shepherd
That You know me so well
There is nothing to shock You
No news I could tell
Yet still You are willing
And ready to lead
What a lesson in mercy
In grace and in deed.

Phil. 2:13
For it is God who works in you,
both to will and to work for his good pleasure

The Good Shepherd Seeks

Sunday Morning

It's the unpredictability
That causes life to spin
When we wake to see the damage
Precious souls are now in
For I did not see this coming
I don't know where this leads
But I know You are in it
Though my humbled heart bleeds
Thank You Father- such kindness
I could never conceive
Unmerited favour
Too rich to believe
Every morning with dawning
Mercy comes with the sun
And you always are faithful
To complete what's begun
So now with ears open
Hearts softened, eyes clear
For Your glory please use this
And draw many hearts near.

Lamentations 3:22-23
The steadfast love of the Lord never ceases,
his mercies never come to an end;
they are new every morning;
great is your faithfulness.

Waiting

I told them, I showed them
I lead them and yet
How quickly, completely
How well they forget
They turned and they ran
And they're still running now.
I can't comprehend it
Or understand how
So now I regroup and I make a fresh start
I surrender my plans
And my tired old heart
And forgetting the past as You told me to do
I hand it all over and give them to You
For it's You Who are saving
It's You Who redeems
Fix my eyes upon You
And breathe hope in my dreams…
I hear You now saying
"This is something I do.
Think back to the times
I have waited for you."

Lamentations 3:24-26
"The Lord is my portion," says my soul,
"therefore I will hope in him."
The Lord is good to those who wait for him,
to the soul who seeks him.
It is good that one should wait quietly
for the salvation of the Lord.

August Third

August third and not one word
When there should have been many
Thoughts and worries fill my head
I cannot confirm any
But You my Heavenly Father know
And see each beating heart
And sometimes waiting patiently
Can be the noblest part.
For living out the nightmares
Or assuming that they're true
Does not seem to honour
Everything I know of You.
So here again I lay them down
Help me shed this cloak of fear
They are Yours and I am trusting
In Your goodness reigning here.
Let this "no news" become "good news"
As I learn to trust in You
Knowing You chose this path for me
As You work their story through.

Isaiah 26:3,4
*You keep him in perfect peace
whose mind is stayed on you,
because he trusts in you.
Trust in the Lord forever,
for the LORD God is an everlasting rock.*

More Thanks

Thank You Lord for keeping us
In all the reckless flow
When we did not consider
Where that next step could go
Thank You for holding us
When dark night set in
And we had no idea
Of the danger we were in
Thank You for seeking us
When we marched away
In our arrogant carelessness
In those darkened days
Thank You for shepherding
Your stubborn sheep through
When we so little cared
What we were doing to You.

Isaiah 53:6
All we like sheep have gone astray;
we have turned—every one—to his own way;
and the Lord has laid on Him the iniquity of us all.

On trusting the Good Shepherd

Elegy

As the last light fades away
The last petal falls
What will they remember
What will they recall
Will they think with fondness
What will memories hold
As time marches forward
And my lifeblood goes cold
In my waning history
Though achievements may be few
May those thoughts that linger
Turn their thoughts to You.

2 Thessalonians 3:5
*May the Lord direct your hearts
to the love of God
and to the steadfastness of Christ.*

Let Them

When I began to grasp
Just what the Saviour did for me
I clearly came to know
A soul's response would have to be
The very same acceptance
Of forgiveness and of grace
For no one could refuse after
That glimpse of Jesus' face.
So when I pray for other souls
Who wander lost on earth
I pray He'd make them see how much
He paid and what they're worth
That they'd know the world's treasures
Are all empty, void and null
And what our Saviour offers is
Real life both rich and full.
Lord let their ears be opened,
And let their blind eyes see
Let them glimpse Your beauty,
Just the way You did for me.

John 6: 44
No one can come to me
unless the Father who sent me draws him.
And I will raise him up on the last day.

On trusting the Good Shepherd

Where Are You Going?

O little sheep tell me where you are going;
Where are you headed; what path do you take?
Do you not hear that Your Shepherd is calling?
You need to come home; it's His heart you break.
Why are you running away from Your Father?
What do you think this world can provide?
Off you go wandering, eyes closed and ears deafened,
Looking for someone to stay by your side.
O how I fear for these little sheep wandering
Time keeps on marching and time does not wait.
How my heart cries for these little sheep wandering
Who need to come home now before it's too late.
Good Shepherd You know our hearts are so heavy
Seeing them living with danger so near
Give us resilience to keep our hope in You
You Who says, "Courage, keep faith and don't fear."
I'm sorry, I'm weary, I'm tired of asking
I'm sad and I'm angry, I'm sick of the fight
Let me shine Your love, Your joy and Your mercy
So I attract them to Your Holy light.
Let me be part of their story of rescue
Standing on promises found in Your Word
Silent when needed and speaking when prompted
Knowing it's Your voice that needs to be heard.

Luke 19:10
*For the Son of Man came
to seek and save the lost.*

You and the World

"Grin and bear it," says the world
As this one spins to madness.
Nail-pierced hands outstretched to us,
You offer peace and gladness
"Find your own way,"
Says the world
Ears deaf and eyes both blind.
"I am the Way, the Truth, the Life.
In Me the road you'll find."
"Live for the moment,"
Says the world
"Just eat, drink and be merry."
"Do what you can for every man
The burdens I will carry."
The world says,
"You'll be rich and free
If you get lots of stuff."
You say, "I am all you need.
I truly am enough."
For all the lambs out wandering
Lost, like I used to be,
Our Shepherd Who seeks out all of us
Has paid the Finder's Fee.

Jeremiah 9:23,24
*Thus says the Lord: "Let not the wise man boast in his wisdom,
let not the mighty man boast in his might, let not the rich man boast in his riches,
but let him who boasts boast about this, that he understands and know me,
that I am the Lord who practices steadfast love, justice, and righteousness in the earth.
For in these things I delight, declares the Lord.*

On trusting the Good Shepherd

Mr. Robin Freewill

I saw a robin still hanging about
Wishing he'd left with the others no doubt
Wondering why he ignored the old prod,
Now feeling frightened, excited and odd.
So now he has choices-decisions to make:
Should he leave right now and which route should he take?
What are his chances if he goes or he stays?
Why does he have to go south anyway?
"Just cuz the others take off every fall
Does not mean that I have to leave-not at all.
I'm sure I can make it. I'm sure I'll be fine.
I do have the option: the choice is all mine."
O Robin Freewill, the things you don't know
Those things called ice storms and blizzards of snow.
O Robin Freewill I know how you think
But I know the price of that liberty drink.

Luke 9:25
*For what does it profit a man
if he gains the whole world
and loses or forfeits himself?*

To Wandering Lambs

Such a Friend Who remains with me
Yet always goes before
Who shows the way to travel
Then meets me at the door
Who never leaves me lonely
Who knows the path I roam
Then comes to bear the baggage
As He turns me back toward Home.
Such a friend is Your Friend
Though you won't acknowledge Him
He offers hope and sunlight
For He knows your eyes are dim
He offers strength and wisdom
He's already paid the fare

On trusting the Good Shepher

He doesn't have to find you
For He's with you everywhere
Yet someday time will run out
It will simply be too late
It weighs my heart down heavy
To see how long you make Him wait
For each season passes faster
As this craft of life sails on
And you have to have a Captain
For the seas we sail upon
I am sad that though we share so much
There is One that you refuse
For though you win earth's gold and riches
Without Him you still lose.

James 5:20
Let him know that whoever brings back a sinner
from his wandering
will save his soul from death
and will cover a multitude of sins.

The Good Shepherd is Born

Underneath the Tree

Heart's hope, soul's joy, peace like a river
Freely and lovingly sent by the Giver
You Who make mountains and fashion the seas
Give to Your children most generously
For You know the burdens that each of us bear
Your deep compassions will meet us all there
Hope for Your children, with fears in their lives
The heart crushing feeling as bad news arrives
Sorrow from lives lived with ugly oppression
Bitterness, anger their constant possession
Sparkling glitter and tinsel on trees
Only a frosting on sorrows like these
We all need compassion as sweeping as Yours
Deep, blood-red fount of forgiveness that pours
From our Redeemer to heal up the past
Author and Finisher, the First and the Last.
Make me Your messenger, let my life speak
Ministering grace to the lost and the weak.

2 Corinthians 1:5
For as we share abundantly in Christ's sufferings,
so through Christ, we share abundantly in comfort too.

Hope

There is a hope that comes with Christmas
That is often masked with greed
As we're tripped up with traditions
And all the things we think we need
And although there's disappointment
After all the gifts are given
Hope returns next Christmas season
And we'll once again be driven
But the end of Revelation
Shows the day we truly seek
Joy from sorrow, peace from trials
No one sick or lost or weak.
It's Your Kingdom come in glory
Here to stay with Christ our King
And that tiny glimpse at Christmas
Is the hope of all You'll bring
For eternity is planted
In our hearts and deep, we know
That our joy comes when Your will
Is done in Heaven and earth below.
And You do not chide Your children
Though we're oh so slow to see
Every glint and ray of glory
Is a glimpse of life with Thee.

Matthew 6:10
*Your kingdom come, your will be done,
on earth as it is in heaven.*

On trusting the Good Shepherd

This Christmas

The Christmas season has returned
And here is what I've almost learned
That all the wrappings, tree and trim
Likely mean much less to Him.
I do my best to celebrate
And while the gifts and lights are great
I'm thinking that I miss the goal
Of praise and worship, heart and soul
So now before more rushing wild
I'll ask the King, Who was that child
To light my heart and trim my mind
So this year when He looks He'll find
A peaceful, holy, restful place
That lifts His Name and shines His grace
And I will try as I am able
To give Him better than a stable
Though once again my gift will be
A gift He had to first give me.

Luke 2:20
And the shepherds returned, glorifying and praising God
for all they had heard and seen, as it had been told them.

The Good Shepherd Tends

If I Could

If I could send you one small gift
I'd send you hope, the Spirit's lift
So every moment up ahead
Would shine in glorious gold instead
Gold in His glory that you swim
In waves of knowing joy in Him.
If I could send you one more prayer
It'd be that you could see Him there
As clearly as you see your hand
And somehow that you'd understand
That every step of this dark way
Is leading to His Glorious Day.
I'd lift you past your grief and pain
And give you back your strength again
And all these days and weeks would be
A distant faded memory
I'd take the weight of hours and days
And heal your mind with songs of praise
To where you'd say, with backward glance
I'm glad I didn't miss the chance
To see the good that came to be
Because He worked those things through me.
And meantime while we wait and pray
The way you trust, the things you say
Are bringing glory to our King
And that's worth more than anything.

2 Corinthians 4:15
*For it is all for your sake, so that as grace extends to more and more people
it may increase thanksgiving, to the glory of God.*

Sitting With Mary

Sitting with Mary in the garden of prayer
Finding Your presence lifting strife and care
Laying them down and finding You are near
Prayers that are spoken and those no one else hears.
Little girl lying in a hospital bed
Cloak her in peace and strength, remove fear and dread
You understand everything Your Mary bore
You will lift spirits as You've done before
Precious mom waiting hoping things go well
Speak to her comfort that no doctors can tell
Pour down refreshing so her spirits rise
You our kind Shepherd, gentle, merciful, wise.
Resting on Jesus taking moments apart
Waiting for quiet to calm troublesome heart
Heavenly Father what a comfort I find
Lightened in spirit and renewed in mind.

John 14:27
Peace I leave with you; my peace I give to you.
Not as the world gives do I give to you.
Let not your hearts be troubled,
neither let them be afraid.

On trusting the Good Shepher

Watching Jessica

When I look at you with my own eyes
That have watched you for so long
I do not see limitations
As though something has gone wrong.
I see dignity and beauty
And a flowing peaceful grace
I see calm and utter stillness
When I look into your face.
I know Jessica you realize
Jesus holds you in His arms
And whatever storms are brewing
There's no reason for alarm
You know every single moment
You rest safely in His gaze
You're a little lamb He carries
And He will though all your days.

Matthew 11:25, 26
At that time Jesus declared,
"I thank you, Father, Lord of heaven and earth,
that you have hidden these things
from the wise and understanding
and revealed them to little children;
yes, Father, for such was you gracious will.

Sand

I have sand from both the oceans
Kept safely in a jar
Two foreign fellows gathered
And full marvelous they are
And one has travelled eastward
And one has travelled west
But neither travelled both ways
To tell me which is best
Yet with the help of others
I can hold both in my hand
And I raise it to my Father
Ask Him to unify this land
Hear Your children who are calling
As we humbly bow this day
We need Your healing and forgiveness
Draw our hearts to You we pray.

2 Chronicles 7:14
*If my people who are called by my name
humble themselves, and pray and seek my face
and turn form their wicked ways,
then I will hear from heaven
and will forgive their sin and heal their land.*

On trusting the Good Shepher

Tender Gaze

Your tender gaze stays steady on
Fragile soul who meets Your dawn
Sun of Righteousness will rise
Healing wings through Heaven's skies
Glorious reigning sovereign Friend
Mercy pouring without end
Agnes facing Heaven's door
Moving closer than before
Sweep her up on angel wings
Let her hear eternal things
Whispered through the brightening air
As they swoop to meet her there
Let her grasp, as earth lets go
Things that soon her heart will know
Joy of being evermore
Safely landed on that shore
On earth, we have not eye nor ear
To fathom life with You so near
Like baby safe in womb of mother
We cannot comprehend another
We with feet bound to this sphere
Cannot grasp life away from here
But tune her heart
To hear those strains
Of Heavenly music as she gains
The right of passage to Your throne
Till her heart sings songs with Your own.

Psalm 116:15
Precious in the sight of the Lord is the death of his saints.

Us and Them

Us and them
Rich and poor
Found and lost
Less and more
Having much, having naught
Unaware of all we've got.
Slow and bright
Mean and kind
Not what you'd
Expect to find
Vision good
But oh so blind
Blinded by
All we claim
Try to duck
And dodge the blame
World gone mad
Sick with rot
Crippled by how much we've got
Eyes to open as we give
Heart to soften, life to live.

Luke 6:24,25
But woe to you who are rich,
for you have received your consolation.
Woe to you who are full now,
for you shall be hungry.

On trusting the Good Shepher

The Big Prayers

The Big Prayers, The Large Needs
The Hours that Bring us Trouble
The Heart Aches, The Sick Souls
The Dreams that Fall to Rubble
The Huge Storms, The Long Nights
The Days that Know No End
The Seasons of Loneliness
Without a Single Friend
The Deep Hurts, The Lost Loves
The Child without a Mother
The Midnight Depression
That Brings a Heaviness to Smother.
Our Answer, Our Solution
The Saviour from Man's Sorrow
Is Christ Who Remains the Same
Every day and each tomorrow
In every predicament
In every single failing
Our Jesus is the Answer
For everything that's ailing
Praise Him that every day
From birth and past the grave
Our High Priest, Our Redeemer
Is Mighty to Save.

I Hebrews 13:8
Jesus Christ is the same yesterday and today and forever.

Some Hurts

Some hurts don't show on the outside
Some wounds don't leave a mark
Some ailments just stay lurking
Inside: deep and dark.
Sometimes we have to take wounds
To the Surgeon of ours souls
For sometimes it's only Jesus
Who can heal and make us whole.
Precious Lord let me remember
Every single soul I meet
Likely bears a secret sorrow
Only You can clearly see.
Grant me grace to share with others
Who are with me on this road
And be willing just to listen
And to help lighten their load.

Galatians 6:2
Bear one another's burdens, and so fulfill the law of Christ.

On trusting the Good Shepher

Beyond The Waiting Room

We are waiting in this little room
To hear what lies ahead
We are threatened with discouragement
That comes with fear and dread.
They say that what is coming
Is a hard place or a rock
And we're bracing to encounter it,
As we bend to meet the shock.
But Your Word and now Your Spirit
Speak of quite a different story
For these mountains and these valleys
Are all ways to shine Your glory
For You'll carry all our burdens
As we cast them one by one
And through Your kindness and deliverance
We can magnify Your Son.
We know that we cannot be sure
Of what could come tomorrow
But we know that You are greater than
Any tragedy or sorrow
So while we're waiting here and wondering
How this chapter will play out
You stream eternal rays of glory
Beyond the shadows and the doubt.

Isaiah 40:5
*And the glory of the Lord shall be revealed,
and all flesh shall see it together,
for the mouth of the Lord has spoken.*

Dark Days

Sometimes when I wake
The day is darker than the night
Every noise a piercing thunder
Knives in every ray of light
And I move along with caution
As though my soul could split in two
As if every step could rupture
All I say or see or do.
And with the pain of living
Comes a dark oppressive crowd
That hums themes of dread and failure,
With a bleak and threatening cloud.

On trusting the Good Shepher

Yet, You always see me through it
And You stay and hold my hand
And I know that I am in
A wondrous strange and hallowed land
Because when the storm has ended
And Your dawn brings healing wings
I am deeply fiercely grateful
For every ordinary thing.
And since You've walked me through the valleys
I have that comforting to share
With my fellow suffering travelers
Who also need Your tender care.

2 Corinthians 1:3, 4
Blessed be the God and Father of our Lord Jesus Christ,
the Father of mercies and God of all comfort,
who comforts us in all our affliction,
so that we may be able to comfort those
who are in any afflictions,
with the comfort with which we ourselves
are comforted by God.

Your Suffering Children

Your suffering children need You Father
Need You in a mighty way
Every time I think about them
Help me pause so I can pray.
Pray Your power strong and mighty
Ends the terrors that they face
Ends the dark and fierce oppression
Brings them hope wrapped up in grace.
Give them strength to stand with courage
Holding fast to all You are
Let them know You never leave them
Let them know You're never far.
Your suffering children need deliverance
Hurting souls need to be free
Your salvation and redemption
Only way that this could be.
So I lift up suffering children
Ask You to clothe them in Your power
Show Your strength and mercy to them
In this dark and evil hour.
One voice crying for a nation
Still I use my voice to plea.
Through the glory of Your Jesus
I know that You're hearing me.

2 Thessalonians 1:4
*Therefore we ourselves boast about you in the churches of God
for your steadfastness and faith
in all your persecutions and in the afflictions
that you are enduring*

On trusting the Good Shepher

At Life's Ebb

Let me be an autumn leaf
As my days are ending
Glorious with all You give
In winds of mercy bending
Dancing to eternal themes
Laughing with the splendor
Tumbling in a brilliant waltz
In ultimate surrender
Colours all heaped one on one
As Your grace keeps pouring
Finishing this earthly march
Till this soul goes soaring.
Life's ebb meets flow happily
Earth's robes now exchanged
Slipping death's gates easily
This globe now old and strange.
May watchers know I did not fear
The path of my demise
For Mercy changed its colours
And I saw with new life's eyes.
If they do not know You Lord
Let them yearn to find
You, my gentle Shepherd Who
Is tender, good and kind.

1 Corinthians 15:55
"O death, where is your victory?
O death, where is your sting?"

Here I Am

The service You've requested
One that honours You our King
Is to loose chains of injustice
To set the captives free
To share food with the hungry
Giving shelter to the poor
Clothing homeless, freeing prisoners
All those things we've seen before
For we all were lost and wandering
In a desperate lonely plight
So we serve You best dear Saviour
When we lead them to Your light.
We'll be builders and restorers
As the captured we release
Then our darkness shines like noonday
As they meet our Prince of Peace.

Isaiah 58:10

*If you pour yourself out for the hungry
and satisfy the desire of the afflicted,
then shall your light rise in the darkness
and your gloom be as the noonday.*

On trusting the Good Shepherd

The *Good* Shepherd Guides

Housekeeping

I keep my house as I keep my mind
I do work hard but I'm mostly blind
Or I'm overwhelmed by the surging mess
So I just keep moving to make it less.
There are closets locked where I dare not go
There are lofts and attics above, below
And I'm overtaken by all that's there
So I step outside where there's fresher air.
But I'm seeing now with a learning eye
That I cannot live under bluer sky
Till I get some help with the hoarded stuff
As I see it now I shout, That's enough!
I want roots-up change, from the stem to stern
And I thank You Lord, though I'm slow to learn
That Your deep commitment to bring me through
Is at work in me, making me like You.
So Lord, here's my house, feeble mind and soul
To submit to You is now my goal
Though I'll take it back thinking I know best
If I'd just stay close, You will do the rest.

Psalm 139:23,24
Search me, O God, and know my heart!
Try me and know my thoughts!
And see if there be any grievous way in me,
and lead me in the way everlasting!

How Long?

O how weary You must be
Of my frail humanity
After all I've learned and seen,
What could ever come between
You and my desire to stay,
What could tempt my heart away?
Even from my early days,
I knew that I owed You praise
For the streams of love You poured,
I did not earn, could not afford
Such a desperate soul am I,
How long does this take, I cry
Till my wandering heart stays still,
Always only in Your will?
Wanting to be gentle, kind,
What must still be in my mind
That is nothing like my King.
I am sickened by this thing
Forbearing and longsuffering too,
Waiting while I stray from You

Drawing me with outstretched hand,
Love I cannot understand.
Peace be still, You speak my name,
There is something not the same
Little bit by little bit,
You are coming close to it.
As you grow weary, you release,
Then what I send you brings you peace
And peace brings joy and joy is kind
And so reshapes your heart and mind.
So seeing trouble in your heart
Is a very crucial part
For your willingness for Me
To do this needed surgery.
Now you'll trust the things I send
To first remove and then to mend
Your heart and mind till we are one.
I will not stop till that is done.

1 Peter 1:6,7
*In this you rejoice, though now for a little while,
if necessary, you have been grieved by various trials,
so that the tested genuineness of your faith—more precious than gold
that perishes though it is tested by fire
—may be found to result in praise and glory
and honor at the revelation of Jesus Christ*

What's Mine Is Yours

I've seen it more than I can say
How You've stepped in and saved the day
And turned my storm clouds into sun
I've watched You flip them one by one
I've heard Your call to turn to You
To forfeit false and turn to true
I've heard Your pleas to seek Your face
And as I've turned You've poured out grace
And dreams and hopes I've held for years
Were born, and dried up dreads and fears.
I cannot count the times You reach
And rescue me and then You teach
My trembling heart to count on You
You're always faithful, always true
But now I sense there's something more
Than things I've learned to ask You for;
As I sit safe behind my doors
You say come out and help with Yours.

Matthew 28:19,20
Go therefore and make disciples of all nations,
baptizing them in the name of the Father
and of the Son and of the Holy Spirit,
teaching them to observe all that I have commanded you.
And behold, I am with you always, to the end of the age.

On trusting the Good Shepher

Lamentations

When I skipped this time
When I missed a day
When I didn't slow down
Enough to pray
Did You sigh for me
Did You shake Your head
As those other things
Filled my day instead?
For You knew my need
For that day now past
And it would have helped
If I'd paused and asked
But tomorrow dawns
With a fresh clear start
With compassions new
From Your faithful heart
So I'll do my best
To do my part
To seek Your help
From the very start.

Matthew 6:8
Do not be like them,
for your Farther knows what you need
before you ask Him.

Bird Song

Calm grey day after storms are spent
Birds returning, wonder where they went
Sweet birds singing of all You are
With silence ringing, it carries far.
Do they sing only as I pause
Where's their rule book and where their laws?
Is it written beneath their wings
Is it joy that just bursts and sings?
Show me roads to that peaceful place
Where I sing as I meet Your grace
Not some chore I'm supposed to do
But simply shining love back to You.

Psalm 145:21
My mouth will speak the praise of the Lord,
and let all flesh bless his holy name forever and ever.

Life Sweeps In

Life sweeps in and I feel small
No chance to endure it all
None to catch me as I fall
Sorrow, no release.
Swirling like a rootless limb
Strains of triumph grown dim
Eyes and ears are needing Him.
He is not found here.
While I'm paralyzed with fear
Feeling all alone down here
Dread for ones that I hold dear
You must rescue.
I stand still and cast on You
These cares as You told me to
Hope begins to rise anew
Peace comes pouring.
Once again my soul will lift
Finding now this priceless gift
You will shepherd hearts that drift
Gracious Father.

1 Peter 5:7
Casting all your anxieties on him,
because he cares for you.

To Constantly Pray

To constantly pray: to pray without ceasing
Means handing things over and freely releasing
Those things that cause worry or anguish or stress
Relinquishing rights and my old selfishness.
It sometimes means raising my face to the skies,
When nothing makes sense and I can't figure why.
To pray without ceasing I'd consistently bring
My good times and bad times to You my kind King.
But really quite often I handle things first
Or I skip the untidy, the messy, the worst.
Yet if I'm to do this, the way this must go
I'd just hand things back, for You already know
And You're never surprised or confused or dismayed.
You know how I work and You know how I'm made
And You have the resources to make all things good
With a new golden value, not stubble or wood.
So You clearly warned us that troubles will come
However we get them, wherever they're from
And our highest objective, what pleases You best
Is to trust each thing to You, to trust You then rest.
And while we are trusting, our thoughts turn to praise
As we see You manage our nights and our days.

1 Thessalonians 5:17,18
Pray without ceasing, give thanks in all circumstances;
for this is the will of God in Christ Jesus for you.

On trusting the Good Shepher

In the Mess

Sometimes this life changes, switching lanes so fast
I cannot be certain that my heart will last
Choices made by others change the course of life
Days of joy and blessing turn to nights of strife
As my heart resumes its beating haltingly
I see my only option is to cast on Thee
Every soul I care for and leave all with You
Knowing You have promised to see all this through
I have not the wisdom that I need right now
Cannot start to fathom this thing any how
Things that I would wish for likely aren't Your best
Drawing hearts to Your heart is my real request
Whether news seems happy or brings deep despair
I can always know that You're already there
What to pray for answers I can't even guess
Just to bring You glory from this present mess.

James 1:5
*If any of you lacks wisdom, let him ask God,
who gives generously to all without
reproach, and it will be given him.*

Nothing Wasted

Nothing wasted, not one breath
From first at birth till last at death
Joy and sorrow, comfort, pain
All is used then used again
We get comfort so we give
Dying teaches how to live
Getting teaches how to share
Find life's lessons everywhere
Eyes to see and ears to hear
You make all things very clear
Everything you send to me
My living sacrifice to Thee.

2 Corinthians 1:3,4
*Blessed be the God and Father
of our Lord Jesus Christ,
the Father of mercies and God of all comfort,
who comforts us in all our affliction,
so that we may be able to comfort those who are in any afflictions,
with the comfort with which
we ourselves are comforted.*

On trusting the Good Shepherd

Being Still

I wanted to shine, I wanted to shimmer
My light to be brighter, not duller and dimmer
But thoughts that I spoke, the words that I said
Were critical, cutting, and cranky instead.
But this passing moment did not surprise You
For You saw it coming. You sent warnings too.
Oh how many flaws still course through my veins
That I keep revealing again and again
Teach me to be still, re-surrender my heart
To be still and be silent would make a good start
Yet in biting my tongue, I might seem to be wise
Yet if You don't remodel, it is just a disguise.
So, place guards at my mouth, and seal my lips tight
For now, that's the way I can get this thing right.
And as I am stifled and my options are narrowed
You my Kind surgeon can divide joint and marrow.

Psalm 141:3
*Set a guard, O Lord, over my mouth;
keep watch over the door of my lips!*

Next Sunday

I went to Church this Sunday
But I didn't see You there
And someone took my favourite spot
And that did not seem fair.
We sang some newer choruses
I like the old ones more
And I much prefer the ushers
To walk me from the door.
The message didn't work for me
I heard nothing new today
The jokes were not as funny
I'm sad to have to say
No one said a word to me
They hardly ever do

You'd think in all the years I've come
Someone could say hello to you
It's good of me to volunteer
To pop in Sunday Morn
I always try to look my best
Not tired, scared and worn
It kind of dampens Sundays
Seeing people look so sad
For no one else has ever had
The troubles I have had
But I'll try again next Sunday
For I'm the optimistic type
It's just the sermon and the worship
And the people that aren't right.

Hebrews 10:25
Not neglecting to meet together, as is the habit of some,
but encouraging one another;
and all the more as you see the Day drawing near.

No Longer

No longer am I waiting
For some big sacrifice
For some monumental moment
That will take me by surprise
But what I think is better
Is to watch along the way
For those little gems to bring to You
Throughout each and every day
Things like serving when I'm weary
Or not speaking when I'm cross
Releasing my stuff freely
Without seeing it as loss
Giving each occasion
That I see a chance to share
Knowing every single moment
You are with me in it there
So while I am not off serving Jesus
On some foreign mission
For now it's still of value
To give You my permission
To take whatever I have got
For it's all Yours anyway
And it marks it with eternity
To give it all away.

Galatians 6:9
Let us not grow weary of doing good,
for in due season we will reap, if we do not give up.

One Thing

This one thing I know
Of this thing I am certain
That life on earth is clouded o're
We live behind a curtain
And the things that seem so sure
And stable and unchanging
Are often in a moment gone
The story's re-arranging
This one thing I've seen
There's one thing I can count on
The things I thought were mine alone
That all my hopes could mount on
Can never be relied upon
They slip between my fingers
And in a flash they're simply gone
A memory only lingers
You know that life on earth
Is only for a season
You warn us not to cling
And claim things for this reason
Time is a slippery slope
A heart beat and it's gone
You are the only One
To build a life upon

James 4:14
Yet you do not know what tomorrow will bring.
What is your life? For you are a mist
that appears for a little time and then vanishes.

Of Lazarus The Beggar

It's easier so it's harder
It's closer so it's far
It's dressed up in tradition
So we can't see where we are
We are blinded so we're wandering
And the path is masked and dim
And our wealth and our possessions
Mean we're not so close to Him
We have more so we have less
We have less so we are lost
And our comfort in the present
Means we'll pay a larger cost
I do not want to have missed it
When I get to Heaven's gate

I don't want to understand this
Then find out that it's too late.
So I'll serve the frail and needy
And give my stuff to help the poor
For there's not a single earthly thing
That fits through Heaven's door.
I want to be kind and sweet and cheerful
I want to be gentle calm and true
I want to reflect my Saviour Shepherd
By the things I say and do
I want to be self controlled and patient
I want to be faithful to the end
I need to stay quietly by Jesus
So you will see my glorious friend.

Luke 16:25

*But Abraham said, "Child, remember that you
in your lifetime received your good things,
and Lazarus in like manner bad things;
but now he is comforted here, and you are in anguish.*

The Question

How do You stand our prayers
When they are praying from a shack
When it's food and clothes and water
That Your other children lack
Mercy that You listen as we ask so much for "me"
When You have to want to cry out
Can't you hear and feel and see?
Are we still so wrapped up in the things
That we still think we need
When so much of it amounts to
Only selfishness and greed?
Small wonder we need to kill the old man
Kill that old man every day
I'm beginning now to see that
There is no other way
This is not just tea and crumpets
There is all out war to fight
And it's only while this heart beats
That we get to get this right.

Romans 7:24
*Wretched man that I am! Who will deliver me
from this body of death?*

On trusting the Good Shepher

Noah's Lesson

In this world you will have trouble
Don't hold this one hard and fast
For it all is passing by us
Nothing here is going to last
And the leaving and the losing
Is much harder when we cling
Life is only ours to borrow:
Vital lesson in this thing.
You are not a God Who frowns upon
Those things that bring us joy
But you understand the system
That this universe employs
This is really quite essential
Life is Yours, it's not our own
There is nothing here that's ours
Everything is here on loan.
So Lord help unclench my fingers
Loosen grip and arms relax.
Heart and mind begin to fathom
These unquestionable facts.
Make us ready for each new day
Knowing You're already there
And those things entrusted to us
Are entrusted so we'll share.

2 Peter 3:11
Since all these things are thus to be dissolved,
what sort of people ought you to be
in lives of holiness and godliness.

A Bird Cannot

A bird cannot help but sing her song
To glorify her Maker
Nor a flower choose the dress she wears
To praise her kind Creator
A rolling river will weave his way
To the Source from which he came
The stallion gallops to extol
His wondrous Sculptor's Name
For everything that's touched by You
Cannot help but shine Your glory.
But mankind made in Your image
Tells a very different story.
For You've given us the option:
We can choose to walk away

And we have a choice in how we live
And what we do and say.
And the dreadful price of freedom
That You paid for our lost souls
Came because we looked to other things
To try to make us whole.
And You had to go to Calvary
Because we all chose to roam
As we lived in full denial
That You are our only home.
So, when we're finally raised to see
What creation lives to sing
May it bless Your heart and bring You joy
When we choose to praise our King.

Ephesians 2:8,9
*For by grace you have been saved through faith.
And this is not your own doing;
it is the gift of God, not a result of works,
so that no one may boast.*

Not Just Good Enough

Not just good enough
Not okay
Not just making it
Through another day
More like looking for
Every place to serve
Knowing everything
Is less than You deserve.
Not just busy-ness
Filling up each hour
More like listening
Moving in Your power.
Much less hecticness
Much more joy and peace
Helping to get ready
For that Day when struggles cease.

2 Peter 1:19
And we have something more sure,
the prophetic word, to which you will do well to pay attention
as to a lamp shining in a dark place,
until the day dawns and the morning star rises in your hearts

On trusting the Good Shepher

The Ship I'm Sailing

Don't like the ship I'm sailing now
Don't like the wind come crashing
Don't want to stay till harbour's found
Don't like the noise and slashing
Don't want to stay this voyage out
Don't want to hear its thunder
Want peace and joy to drive it on
Want grace and love and wonder
My choices stand quite clear to me
To run or to surrender
To seek the Pilot of the craft
To find His purpose tender.
I'm weary of the journey here
I'm frightened of my failing
I'm lifting eyes to seek Your face
And find Your will prevailing.

1 Peter 2: 19
*For this is a gracious thing, when,
mindful of God, one endures sorrows
while suffering unjustly.*

Through The Valley

Eyes shut, heart closed,
Ears that do not hear
Not remembering
I can find You near.
Not quite ready to
Open hands, release
Mired in misery,
Forfeiting Your peace.
Angry still I steep,
Sunk in waves of scorn
Eyes on darkest night,
Miss Redemption's morn.
Dark bleak space ahead
Must be travelled through
Blind hands fumble for
Yours, to bring me through.
Poisoned stomach pain,
Cold blood pooled in heart

Trapped here far too long:
Bless this feeble start.
I see tiny glints
Of a coming day.
Your arm none too short
Starts to show the way.
Now I stumble forth
You are not so far
As I now recall
The tender God You are.
Into all that is
Steeped and lit with You
Freefall into grace
As You ask me to.
Someday eyes will see
Someday ears will hear.
This day faith exalts
Just to feel You near.

1 Peter 5:10
And after you have suffered a little while,
the God of all grace,
who has called you to his eternal glory in Christ,
will himself restore, confirm, strengthen and establish you.

The Service You've Requested

The service You've requested
One that honours You our King
Is to loose chains of injustice
To set the captives free
To share food with the hungry
Giving shelter to the poor
Clothing homeless, freeing prisoners
All those things we've seen before
For we all were lost and wandering
In a desperate lonely plight
So we serve You best dear Saviour
When we lead them to Your light.
We'll be builders and restorers
As the captured we release
Then our darkness shines like noonday
As they meet our Prince of Peace.

Isaiah 58:12
And your ancient ruins shall be rebuilt;
you shall raise up the foundations of many generations;
you shall be called the repairer of the breach,
the restorer of streets to dwell in.

On trusting the Good Shepher

What Still?

What still you dwell on what is not
And still you miss the things you've got?
Just sit down in Contentment's chair
And see all that I've left you there.
What still expecting even more
Than all the things I've done before?
Take off the cloak of gloom and doubt
And see My blessings all about.
Fling off the old self you still hold
Who blocks your view all shiny gold,
Who causes you to cringe in fear,
Forgetting I'm always near.
Look up and fix your gaze up high
And soon you'll start to wonder why
You chose to walk with eyes cast down
And missed My glory all around.
Let me walk with you little sheep
Then you'll see how I love and keep
And tend My flocks with Shepherd's care
Every moment, everywhere.

Hebrews 12:2
Looking to Jesus, the founder and perfecter of our faith,
who for the joy that was set before him endured the cross,
despising the shame
and is seated at the right hand of the throne of God.

I Mean Well

I mean well
I want what's right
I desire to shine
Your Holy Light
To soldier on and the fight the fight
For You are worthy.
I hope to
Express Your love
To sing Your praise
Like gentle dove
To put my heart
In things above
Live for You only.

It's Mercy
And Grace You give
That gives me strength
So I can live
You even help me
Want to live
As Your child.
Praise that
You know my frame
That though I fail
Again, again
I'm still Yours,
You know my name
Forever and ever.

1 Timothy 6:12
Fight the good fight of faith.
Take hold of the eternal life
to which you were called
and about which you made the good confession
in the presence of many witnesses.

Fair and Foul

A fair-weather friend will leave you
When the storm clouds start to show
When you face a sticky problem
That friend will simply go.
A fair-weather friend starts running
When the road gets long or tough
A fair-weather friend's not steady
He says, "I'm off. I've had enough."
But sometimes Lord, I wonder
If I'm much the same to You
But I come just when there's trouble
Wanting help to make it through.
I'm a foul-weather friend I'm thinking
And that's also wrong to be
When I'm only coming to You
To see what You'll do for me.
The true friendship that You long for
Is a friend through all of life
Those who walk the road together
Like a Bridegroom and His wife.

John 15:12, 13
This is my commandment,
that you love one another as I have loved you.
Greater love has no one than this,
that someone lay down his life for his friends.

On trusting the Good Shepherd

So Be Careful

If things were always easy I'd soon think that it was me
That I could handle each day really marvelously
For I'd think that I was acting with admirable strength
And had enough wisdom to cover Life's length
But Life is not easy and its gales blow wild
And I am not the Master but a lonely lost child
And I always need saving like a little lost lamb
And it's when this Life buffets I recall Whose I am
And each time You rescue, set me back on my feet
I'm reminded I need You for every heart beat.

Deuteronomy 6:12
Then take care lest you forget the Lord,
who brought you out of the land of Egypt,
out the house of slavery.

This Carnal Soul

This carnal soul who still resides
Is not some feisty neighbor
Who livens up the quiet parts
And adds spice to life's labour
But rather she's the part that's left
Of hate and scorn and malice
That thief that still has partial rights
Within this Saviour's palace
And somehow it is left to me
To recognize her voice
To bind her up and drag her out
I understand the choice
I must shower in the cleansing flow
Each day and every time
I see the footprints, hear the voice
Of that old soul of mine.
The King of Glory lives within
But sin's soul can still reside
Teach me dear Saviour how to live
A cleansed and holy bride.

2 Cor. 10:5
*We destroy arguments and every lofty opinion
raised against the knowledge of God,
and take every thought captive to obey Christ.*

On trusting the Good Shepherd

One Of Those Days

It's clearly one of those days
When nothing seems to come out right
When it's clouds and mud and bleakness
And the sun stays hid from sight
And I only wanted restfulness
And perhaps a splash of joy
But every single moment
Brings more darkness to destroy.
But no matter who intended them
To turn my thoughts to black
It's my own responsibility
To take steps and send them back.
So I claim this very moment,
And every moment not arrived
To send thanks and spoken gratitude
For each heartbeat I'm alive
For we're on this road together
And the end is drawing near
And my Father God the King of all
Says I never need to fear
So with just this starting baby step,
I turn and voice my praise
That He's sovereign over all my seconds,
Minutes, hours and days.

Philippians 3:1
Finally, my brothers, rejoice in the Lord.
To write the same things to you is no trouble to me
and is safe for you.

The Good Shepherd Leads

On trusting the Good Shepher

Jessica's Rules

Don't complain, in sun or rain
Don't go where you are not
Don't compare with anyone
No matter what they've got
Be happy in the chair you sit
And on the rock you stand
God knows your frame and make-up
And He works a glorious plan
And don't dwell on tomorrow
Be it sunny skies or grey
For in your dread or dreaming
You will miss out on today

1 Timothy 6:6, 7, 8
*Now there is great gain in godliness with contentment
for we brought nothing into the world
and we cannot take anything out of the world.
But if we have food and clothing
with these we will be content.*

The Farther I Go

The farther I go the more I see
My little life's simplicity
For every day is simply this
To watch for You and never miss
The chance to speak of what You've done
Of all I have through Christ Your Son
Our gifts are gifts sent from above
And every trial is sent in love.
The good, the bad, the hard, the sweet
Leads on to triumph, not defeat
For every step of every day
Is mapped ahead to lead the way
To that Great Day when strife is done
And we can see Your victory won
O let my life Your glory tell
And grant me strength to finish well.

2 Timothy 4:2
Preach the word;
be ready in season and out of season;
reprove, rebuke, and exhort,
with complete patience and teaching.

On trusting the Good Shepher

Grant

Grant that I may never stand
In the path of Your great hand
Blocking rays from other's view
So they miss the glimpse of You
May my fears and troubled mind
Never cause a soul to find
Focus on the present strain
Missing grace of Your great Name
Make my path, my heart, my voice
Go rejoicing with the choice
Shining up to Your great throne
Yours the focus, not my own
Only through redeeming Power
Can You transform hour by hour
Even something good I do
To shine glory back to You.

1 Thessalonians 5:16,17,18
Rejoice always, pray without ceasing,
give thanks in all circumstances;
for this is the will of God in Christ Jesus for you.

You and I

Here I sit alone today
No one hearing what I say
No one seeing what I do
No one knowing—only You.
You the Vine and I a leaf
I remain and so receive
Everything I'll ever need
You the Gardener, me the seed
Not a single thing to grieve
All from You I will receive
Orchestrating on this theme
You the Dreamer, me the dream
You the Husband, me the wife
You the Sculptor of my life
Nothing passes from Your view
Everything a gift from You.
Let me bow now at Your throne
My whole life is now Your own
You are sifting as is best
I am grateful, quite at rest.
I am married to You Lord
Woven into golden cord
Trusting You to only move
For Your glory, in Your love.

Colossians 3:17
*And whatever you do,
in word of deed, do everything
in the name of the Lord Jesus,
giving thanks to God the Father through him.*

Little Life Of Mine

Oh this little life of mine
Meted out in one small line
Here and now I do my part
Weary from the end to start
O this glorious life of Yours
Streams of joy and mercy pour
Always there for me to drink
Fuel for every thought I think
O the thought of us combined
You reforming heart and mind
Soul leads hands and feet to tread
Boldly in Your light instead
O this wondrous chance to shine
Rays of glory pour from mine
You enabling little me
To work in Your eternity
Little chores are now made great
I can move not stand and wait
Every day a lavish gift
Yours to change, renew and lift
Oh this little life of mine
A gift most precious and divine
While You strengthen me to live
May I only praises give.

1 Corinthians 15:58
*Therefore, my beloved brothers, be steadfast,
immovable, always abounding in the work of the Lord,
knowing that in the Lord your labor is not in vain.*

Listen a Moment

Listen a moment to what the world teaches
What is it saying to the millions it reaches?
Just so much talent, so little to say
For me it works the other way
So much to say but to get it all said
Write black and white when all of it's red.
So much to tell but no one to hear
So many close but nobody near.
Too much to handle, so little learned
All of it given, none of it earned.
Grace in a teaspoon, offered in flood
Flesh torn and battered, flowing with blood.
Nothing I've earned and nothing deserved
Should have come reigning yet He came and served
So much is given, too much to know
How do I tell it, how can I show?
I know the secret, I hold the key
Until you have eyesight you never will see.
So much to say to get the words out
Whisper and sing it and speak it and shout
Here in this ripple of eternity
You choose to speak through flawed vessels like me.
Here is my lifetime, it's all that is mine.
Make it have meaning, I want it to shine.

Matthew 5:16
In the same way, let your light shine before others,
so that they may see your good works
and give glory to your Father who is in heaven.

I Want To Be

I want to be all this and more
I want to reach the other shore
And know that I have done for You
All the things You've asked me to
I want to hear Your voice and go
Not hesitate but really know
I'm doing things You planned for me
From early on eternity.
A meek disciple in the gale
I fear that if I start I'll fail
I hear the wind, I see the sky
I'll falter, fail You, then I'll die.
"O silly frightened sheep," You call
"This fear is not from Me at all,
Where I send you, I've gone before
And what is better, what is more
We'll walk together side by side
I am the Bridegroom, you the bride.
I give strength and ability
You simply walk along with Me."
I understand this better now.
You are the Why, the When, the How
My part is really very small
I am the shadow, that is all.

Matthew 14:30, 31
But when he saws the wind, he was afraid,
and beginning to sink he cried out, "Lord, Save me,"
Jesus immediately reached out his hand and took hold of him,
saying to him, "O you of little faith, why did you doubt?"

From That to This

It seems when I was younger,
A wee girl still quite little
I rarely got the chance to speak,
As I came in at the middle
With siblings who were older
And more siblings who were small
And with all the commotion
I rarely got a chance at all
Yet as I grew from that to this
The thought has seemed to stay
That we only get a minute
To say what we would say
And it better be important.
It should foster love and peace
For like a fleeting vapor
Opportunity will cease.

Now when I read Scripture
That same concept does appear
That fewer words are better
To make a message clear.
Gushing words can lead to folly.
That's a good thing to avoid
And there's more hope of enriching
When it's less words I've employed
So what once seemed very trying:
Difficult, unfair
Was preparation that I'd need
When I got my chance to share
So, let my deeds be many,
Streaming love for those with less.
But help me choose my words with caution,
To encourage and to bless.

Proverbs 16:24
Gracious words are like a honeycomb,
sweetness to the soul and health to the body.

It's Much More

It's much more than not complaining
It's more than standing strong
It's more than just enduring
All that seems to go so wrong
It's thanksgiving in the moment
It's the sacrifice of praise
It's seeking Your face in it
In those black and frightening days
And as we whisper Thank You
And submit our strife and care
You build faithful steps to stand on
And You meet us closer there.

Hebrews 13:15
*Through him then let us continually
offer up a sacrifice of praise to God,
that is, the fruit of lips that acknowledge his name.*

Ears To Hear

To those with ears to hear
And eyes to see this glow
There is such a perfect logic
To these things we simply know
That each and every sunrise
And the setting of the same
Is a sonnet sent with love
To those who share Your Name
And the world without Your presence
And without Your guiding hand
Is too hard to be imagined,
A place we cannot understand
So, the tricky kind of problem
That Your children often face
Is how to share Your Kingdom
With a soul who knows no grace
But You promise to work through us
Even when it seems bizarre
So our very lives will speak of
The kind Saviour that You are.

1 Peter 3:15
But in your hearts honor Christ the Lord as holy,
always being prepared to make a defense to anyone
who asks you for a reason for the hope that is in you;
yet do it with gentleness and respect.

Three Sprites

Three shadowed sprites slip side by side
Through calm and stormy weather
They steadily proceed along
They're always found together
And in their sure progression
Each sings a different song
And as my stride meets each of theirs
I start to sing along.
One tends to dwell on what went wrong
Of what he could have had
In regretful clothes of mourning
He bemoans the bleak and bad.
One tends to look to things to dread
He wears a cloak of fear

He thinks of what could ruin him
Within the coming year.
Between those two walks someone
Who can choose his own attire
And as he dons his garment
It will shape what will transpire.
For yesterday is over
And tomorrow I can't see
But how I meet today
Could mark eternity.
For Today I'll trust my Shepherd
And He'll banish dread and fear
For He sings of Hope and Joy
As day by day meets year by year.

Matt. 6:33.34

But seek first the kingdom of God and his righteousness,
and all these things will be added to you.
Therefore do not be anxious about tomorrow,
for tomorrow will be anxious for itself.
Sufficient for the day is its own trouble.

This Life is a Funny Place

This life is a funny place
Souls don't often match the face
Spoken words betray the heart
Finish where they didn't start
Miss the things they meant to do
And things they never managed to.
Every day a Shepherd needs
Reining in our words and deeds.
Calling them to bring them home
Steady on, no more to roam
Hearts and hands and voice and feet
Sovereign Author let them meet
Eyes fixed on the Saviour's face
Who beckons home the human race.

1 Samuel 16:7
*But the Lord said to Samuel,
"Do not look on his appearance
or on the height of his stature,
because I have rejected him.
For the Lord sees not as man sees:
man looks on the outward appearance,
but the Lord looks on the heart.*

Dressed For The Day

With the breastplate of Righteousness held in place
By the belt of Truth buckled round my waist
Shield to extinguish those arrows of flame
Helmet shining Victory in the Saviour's Name
Shoes that make me ready to speak of Your Peace
With the Spirit's sword, Your Word I release
In every circumstance alert and in prayer
Knowing My Redeemer will meet me there
Clothed in Your armour, Your Strength and Your Might
I will stand my ground in the Heavenly fight

Ephesians 6:10
*Put on the whole armor of God
that you may be able to stand
against the schemes of the devil.*

Extraordinary

I will not be ordinary
I will not live dark or dull
I will live some great adventure
Every sunrise rich and full.
I won't settle on the low ground
Where the ordinary roam
My life will be rich with flavor
And my story all my own.
Then your Father smiles saying
"I have made you with this dream.
Child of Mine, unlike another
Life is not as it would seem.
As you listen in obedience
In this fold you feel holds tight
I'm preparing great things for you
All I do is good and right
Moses, David, many others
Rose to heights they could not know
First they lived with sheep on hillsides
While I schooled their hearts to grow
So my son do not feel anxious
That these fields will keep you here
Listen, wait and follow closely
And our dream will soon appear."

Psalm 37:3,4
Trust in the Lord, and do good;
dwell in the land and befriend faithfulness.
Delight yourself in the Lord
and he will give you the desires of your heart.

On trusting the Good Shepher

A Mother's Heart

O what a thing a mother's heart
That carries such a load
That shelters tiny heartbeats
As they start this lifelong road
That sits with troubled little souls
Explains life's hows and whys
That needs such careful wisdom
Under ever-changing skies.
That tumbles headlong into love
Then must set those loved ones free
And step aside with earnestness
To see what they will be.
I pray my Gentle Shepherd
That I live life so we see
That they come to follow Jesus
As they first had followed me.

Isaiah 49:15
*Can a woman forget her nursing child,
that she should have no compassion
on the son of her womb?
Even these may forget, yet I will not forget you.
Behold, "I have engraved you on the palms of my hands;
your walls are continually before me.*

On trusting the Good Shepherd

Afterword of Thanks

Not only did You bless me
With a passion for Your Word
Where I simply couldn't get enough
Desiring more, the more I heard
You also gave my pen a gift
So I could write with ease
And I write for fun and happiness
As poems fly in upon a breeze.
And they bring words to encourage me
To help me soldier through
And they seem to do the same
With others who have read them too.
Then You kept on sending messengers
Who urge to share these gifts You've given
As I write the things You're teaching me
About life and death and heaven.
You know every soul You've sent to me
Everything they've said and done
All of us want only this
To share and glorify Your Son.
So, the profit, if there's profit
Will help extend Your will on earth
Welcoming outcast children home to learn
Their great eternal worth.

100% of money raised by this project goes to

Bridge Of Hope Ministry

Gospel for Asia

For more information please go to:
Gospel for Asia
Gfa.ca
Bridge of Hope

The Next Best Thing

Index

The Good Shepherd Provides

The Good Shepherd Seeks

The Good Shepherd is Born

The Good Shepherd Tends

The Good Shepherd Guides

The Good Shepherd Leads

Made in the USA
Charleston, SC
28 April 2014